K Spanker
L Royal
M Upper Top-Gallant
N Lower Top-Gallant

O Upper Top-Sail
P Lower Top-Sail
Q Fore-Sail, Main-Sail
   and Cross-Jack

Series 601

This book tells the story of ships—from the first rough dug-out canoe of primitive man, to the modern passenger liner, container ship and nuclear-powered submarine. The wonderful coloured pictures include the majestic vessels of the great days of sail.

This is a book to thrill the heart of every boy and girl.

The story of
SHIPS

by Richard Bowood
with illustrations by
Robert Ayton

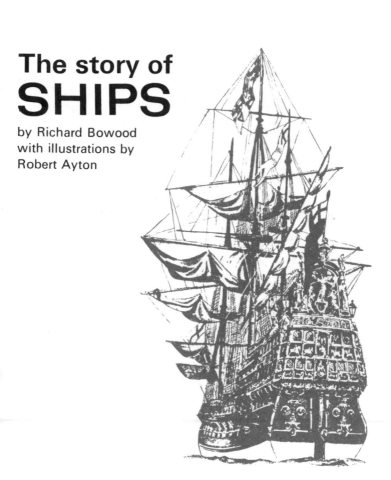

Publishers: Ladybird Books Ltd . Loughborough
© Ladybird Books Ltd (formerly Wills & Hepworth Ltd) 1961
Printed in England

The First Boats

Ships are always beautiful to see. A yacht sailing close-hauled is a splendid sight; so is an ocean liner, a warship, or a cargo boat. When we are young we love to sail model ships, and when we were even younger we liked to have ships in the bath. What greater fun is there than making a ship, or lashing wood together to make a raft, or playing with a rubber raft at the seaside? There is magic about ships.

Man has made himself boats from the earliest times. He began with a log, or several logs lashed together. The earliest settlements were usually beside a river, for it was easier to travel by river than along a dangerous forest path. Boats made fishing easier, too.

One day someone thought of hollowing out a log with fire or stone tools, and gradually the hollowed-out log was shaped with points at the ends to go through the water more easily. Thus the canoe was invented. Canoes used by the primitive people living in remote parts of the world to-day show how the ship was born.

4   *Primitive man afloat*

0 7214 0134 1

The Earliest Ships

Primitive man used boats; the first vessels we know about which were truly *ships* were built more than five thousand years ago by the ancient Egyptians. Their civilisation depended on the navigation of the River Nile and the eastern Mediterranean, and we know about their ships from the wall paintings and models in their royal tombs.

The ships of ancient Egypt had twenty or more oarsmen on each side, but they also had a mast to take a square sail to be used with a following wind. They were steered by one, or sometimes two, long oars at the stern. Warships had a metal head which was used as a ram to sink an enemy ship.

In ancient Egypt ships were built for ceremonial purposes (for the use of the king), for war, and to carry cargo—for there are pictures of ships carrying cattle and grain. There were very few trees in Egypt, so the shipbuilders could not get long planks and had to use short pieces of wood lashed together.

Ancient Egyptian ship on the Nile

Ships of Ancient Greece

The Phoenicians lived on the eastern coast of the Mediterranean, north of Egypt, and they too used long rowing galleys, with a number of oarsmen and a single sail. The Phoenicians were great traders, and their boats must have been large and sturdy, because they not only traded up and down the Mediterranean, but ventured out into the Atlantic to trade with western Europe and the ancient Britons.

The successors to the Phoenicians as a sea-power were the Greeks. We know about their ships, still of the same type, from accounts in the poems of the classical Greek authors and from the pictures which were painted on vases. These pictures, painted nearly three thousand years ago, show what beautiful and efficient ships the ancient Greeks built. Their warships were long and narrow with a single sail, and capable of being driven at great speed by two, three, or even more banks of oarsmen. The sharp metal rams on the bows could tear an enemy ship apart.

A war galley of ancient Greece

The Fleets of Rome

The Romans used war galleys of the same type as the Greeks, with as many as four or five banks of oars. The oarsmen were situated below deck, with ports for their oars, thus providing a clear deck for the soldiers. When the Roman Empire was firmly established, however, merchant ships became more important than war galleys.

The Romans used small, sturdy sailing ships, with plenty of beam to make room for the cargo. There was a cabin aft, and a high, carved stern-post. A small foresail was added, rigged right forward beyond the prow, which greatly improved the ship's sailing qualities.

These Roman ships sailed between Rome and the ports of her Empire, which spread over all Western Europe and included Britain, carrying supplies for her armies and taking back corn and produce to Rome. It was a ship of this kind in which St. Paul sailed and was wrecked off the coast of Malta, as you can read in the two last chapters of "The Acts of the Apostles".

A Roman ship

Viking Long Ships

If you had been living near the coast of England a thousand years ago, you would have dreaded the 'Dragon Ships' of the Vikings. This warlike race came from Norway and Denmark to make terrible raids on our coasts; to murder, pillage and burn.

We know about these ships from the old Norse sagas, and actual examples can still be seen. The Vikings buried their chieftains in large mounds with their ships. When a mound was excavated at Gokstad in Norway a ship was found wonderfully preserved.

They were long, slender ships with beautiful lines. The Gokstad ship had sixteen oars on each side, a stern oar for steering, and, as in Egyptian, Phoenician, Greek and Roman Ships, a mast for a square sail. The shields of the warriors were hung along the sides of the ship. In these beautifully built Dragon Ships the Vikings crossed the North Sea to raid Britain, sailed into the Mediterranean, and even crossed the Atlantic Ocean to America.

A Viking 'Dragon Ship'

The First Ocean Ships

The long open galley, with oars and a square sail to be set when the wind was favourable, remained for hundreds of years. It was in galleys like this that the Normans came to invade England in 1066. Sailing ships were used in the Middle Ages, but they were slow and cumbersome and had to depend on a following wind.

Important changes came in the fifteenth century. Ships were given rudders instead of steering oars, which meant they had to have blunt sterns. They were built larger, with two, three and even four masts. 'Castles' were built fore and aft to protect fighting men in battle—hence the forecastle, or fo'c'sle, in modern ships.

Mediterranean countries continued to use rowing galleys, but nations using sailing ships found them more efficient and able to cross oceans. In the age of chivalry the sailing ships were very gay, bedecked with heraldic colours and devices, flags, banners and streamers.

A fifteenth century ship

Voyages of Exploration

The larger, sturdier ships, with better sailing qualities and space for stores, made longer voyages possible. At the same time the invention of the ship's compass and discoveries in the science of navigation opened new possibilities. Daring voyages were made into unknown oceans. In 1492 Columbus sailed across the Atlantic and discovered America, and in 1497 Vasco da Gama sailed round the southern tip of Africa, and John Cabot discovered Newfoundland.

In 1514 a famous ship was launched at Woolwich, the pride of King Henry VIII and all Englishmen. She was the *Henri Grace à Dieu*, popularly known as *The Great Harry*. She was the wonder and admiration of her day: 1,500 tons, four masts, towering 'castles', a crew of 907, and armed with 195 guns.

She must have looked magnificent, her hull adorned with intricate carving, painted in gold, red, blue and green, with her flags and banners streaming.

'The Great Harry'

Drake and the Golden Hind

The reign of Queen Elizabeth I (1558-1603) was an age of adventure and discovery. Further improvements in shipbuilding, and in aids to navigation and map-making, set men dreaming. They dreamed of exciting voyages to unknown lands, of wonders and of treasure.

England and Spain were struggling for supremacy of the seas, and English seamen set out to raid Spanish ships, returning from the New World laden with treasure. We called them 'Merchant Adventurers'; the Spaniards called them 'Pirates'!

Daring voyages were made, and the most famous seaman of all was Francis Drake, whom the Spaniards called 'the Devil'. Drake sailed away in 1577 in the *Pelican*, which was only three yards longer than a cricket pitch. In her he sailed round the world. On the voyage he renamed his ship *The Golden Hind*, and when he came back after his three years adventure, laden with Spanish treasure, the Queen knighted him. It was an age of stout ships, brave seamen, and a wonderful spirit of adventure.

'The Golden Hind' at Cape Horn

The Spanish Armada

In the year 1588 England was saved by her ships and seamen. The long struggle between England and Spain reached its climax when a mighty fleet set sail from Spain to conquer England. The Spanish Armada, of a hundred-and-thirty ships, planned to sail up the Channel, fighting off the English fleet; then pick up a Spanish army in the Netherlands, cross to England and vanquish her.

The English fleet, of about the same number of sail, but with smaller ships, lay in wait at Plymouth. It was commanded by Lord Howard of Effingham, with such famous fighting seamen as Sir Francis Drake, Sir Martin Frobisher, and Sir John Hawkins.

It was a running fight for nine days as the English fleet pursued the Spaniards up the Channel until the Armada took shelter in Calais. There they were attacked by six fireships—empty ships full of gunpowder, set alight and sent to drift among the enemy fleet. The final battle was fought off Gravelines, and the great Armada was broken and scattered, and driven to its doom by a strong south-west wind. The mighty sea-power of Spain was smashed.

The great sea-battle of 1588

The Sea Power of England

The defeat of the Spanish Armada settled the question of supremacy between England and Spain, but during the next century conflict continued between England, France and Holland. Exciting voyages of discovery were continued, and trade developed with new lands, whose wealth was brought to Europe by ships.

Shipbuilding and rigging methods improved steadily during the seventeenth century. Men were found to command and man the ships, seamen who could manage the larger and more complicated ships, and who had learned their ways about the oceans.

The kings of England knew the importance of a well-found and well-manned fleet to an island nation, with ever-growing connections of trade with the Old World and the New.

King Charles I built fine ships such as the *Sovereign of the Seas*. Charles II took such an interest in building ships that he became known as the 'Father of the British Navy'. He was ably assisted by Samuel Pepys, the great diarist, who was Secretary to the Admiralty.

'The Sovereign of the Seas' 1637

Captain Cook

In 1768 a small ship of 360 tons set sail from England on a historic voyage. She was *The Endeavour* commanded by Captain James Cook of the Royal Navy. She sailed south-westwards, rounded Cape Horn into the Pacific and so to Tahiti, to make astronomical observations. Then Captain Cook continued westwards and sailed round New Zealand and up the east coast of Australia, proving for the first time that they were great islands. He continued westwards, round the Cape of Good Hope and so home.

This voyage round the world was of the greatest importance, apart from Captain Cook's discoveries. On every long voyage many seamen died from a terrible wasting sickness called scurvy. Captain Cook took special precautions to keep his ship clean and dry, and he made his crew drink orange, lemon or lime juice every day, when fresh vegetables and fruit were not available.

The result was astonishing; not one sailor died on the three years voyage round the world. It was a discovery which was to save the lives of countless sailors in the future.

On board 'The Endeavour'

The Wooden Walls of England

Britain was at war for most of the eighteenth century, and in the constant duty at sea the traditions, discipline and superb seamanship of the Royal Navy were forged. In the many sea-battles it was tempered into the magnificent Service of which we are so proud.

The eighteenth century produced great admirals, captains, officers and men—and great fighting ships built of English oak. At Portsmouth we can still go on board Nelson's *Victory*. We can lean on the solid bulwarks, go below to the decks where the seamen lived and the gunners fired their guns. We can gaze at the great towering masts, the yards, and the intricate pattern of the rigging.

Imagine the courage and skill of the seamen of those days, working on the yards at a dizzy height above the deck to furl sail in a full gale, with the great ship tossing and plunging. Imagine the thunder and crash of battle. Imagine also what a wonderful sight it must have been to see the fleet at sea; masts crowded with sail, flags flying and everything shipshape.

H.M.S. 'Victory' 1805

The Merchantmen

More and more merchant ships sailed the seas as trade with other countries increased. The ships linked Europe with the ancient civilizations of India and China, with the new settlements in America and Canada, Africa, Australia and New Zealand, with the West Indies, and with scattered islands all over the world.

As Great Britain won her world-wide empire, her merchantmen took out our manufactured goods, and passengers, and troops to guard our possessions. The same ships brought back rich cargoes—raw materials for industry and such things as tea, sugar and cotton.

The merchant ships of the eighteenth century were similar to the men-of-war, for it was necessary to be armed in an era of war and pirates. The largest and the finest ships were the East India merchantmen, which sailed between Britain and India. They took out the men who spent their lives developing and organizing that great land, and brought home the riches which made Britain the wealthiest nation in the world.

An East Indiaman

Ocean Greyhounds

The most perfect sailing ships the world has ever seen were the British China tea clippers of a hundred years ago. They were thoroughbred racers from stem to stern, from mast-head to keel. Built like yachts, with sharp-raking bows and tall masts, they raced across half the world, from China to London, with cargoes of tea.

The first tea of a new season's crop fetched the highest price in the London market, so there was great rivalry between the tea shippers. The first cargo home meant a big profit to the merchant; it also meant great honour to the captain and crew.

So the tea clippers raced home with their precious cargoes for a hundred days and more, heeling over with canvas taut through storms, or ghosting silently through calms.

Their very names stir the imagination; *Ariel, Taiping, Thermopylae*, and, most famous of them all, *Cutty Sark*. The *Cutty Sark* has been preserved, and lies at peace at Greenwich, where we can go on board and marvel at her beauty, and dream of the splendour of the days of sail.

'The Cutty Sark'

Paddle-Wheel Steamers

A strange and wonderful vessel was seen on the Forth and Clyde Canal in the year 1801, a ship driven by a steam engine and paddle-wheels. Most people thought the idea no more than a freak, yet it was the sign of great changes to come.

Engineers tackled the many problems of devising steamships and, slowly at first, progress was made. In 1819 the *Savannah* crossed the Atlantic. She used her sails for most of the voyage, but for part of the time her paddle-wheels were driven by a steam engine.

In the year 1838 two steamships arrived in America on the same day, the *Sirius* and the *Great Western*. Neither had used its sails; they had crossed the Atlantic entirely by steam. The *Sirius* had only just managed it, for she had used up all her coal and finished the voyage burning her yards!

More and more steamships propelled by paddle-wheels went into service, but for many years they had masts and sails as well—just to be sure.

The Cunard steamship 'Britannia' 1840

The Blue Riband of the Atlantic

A famous name in the early days of steamships was the *Great Eastern* of 1858. She was five times larger than any other ship afloat; she had a screw as well as paddle-wheels; and she had six masts and five funnels.

The steamship was an established fact. Paddle-wheels were replaced by a screw, or propeller, and in 1845 they began to build ships of iron instead of wood. Many people were astonished at that, for they knew that wood floats and iron sinks! Iron was soon replaced by steel.

Ships became larger and sails were dispensed with, leaving two masts only. Twin screws were introduced, and the steam turbine began to take the place of steam engines. Great rivalry sprang up between the nations for the 'Blue Riband of the Atlantic', the honour awarded to the ship making the crossing in the fastest time.

Britain's greatest pride was the *Mauretania*, launched in 1906. She displaced thirty-two thousand tons and was capable of more than twenty-seven knots. This grand old ship held the 'Blue Riband' for twenty-two years.

Ironclads and Battleships

Paddle-wheels being very vulnerable to attack in battle, the Royal Navy, for a time, remained content with the slow, cumbersome but magnificent sailing men-of-war which had been our glory. When the screw was introduced, however, the Navy adopted steam, and the grand old ships were laid up one by one.

The next step in the development of the fighting ship were the 'Ironclads', wooden hulls cased with iron plates, which were followed by ships with steel armour-plated hulls. The invention of the revolving gun turret, with armament of increasing power and accuracy, brought more changes in design.

In the early years of the twentieth century Germany began to build a large and powerful fleet, challenging Great Britain's world supremacy at sea. The answer was Britain's mighty battleship *Dreadnought*, the most powerful fighting ship then known. *Dreadnought* had ten twelve-inch guns, steam turbines, and a speed of twenty-one knots.

H.M.S. 'Dreadnought' 1914

Queens of the Ocean

The old sailing ships were romantic and beautiful, but they were most uncomfortable. A voyage was slow and uncertain ; food was rough and accommodation crude. A journey across the ocean was something of an ordeal.

Steamships changed all that. A voyage became comfortable and safe. Nations and shipping companies vied with each other to build better and faster ships, and they also tried to outdo each other in providing for the comfort of the passengers.

An ocean liner became a luxury hotel afloat. There were fine cabins and richly furnished lounges. The splendid dining saloons served luxurious food, with an orchestra playing, and fresh flowers on the tables. There were sports decks, swimming pools, theatres and cinemas, and playrooms for children.

Britain took the lead in the world's liners with her magnificent *Queen Mary* and *Queen Elizabeth*, the largest, the fastest and the most luxurious ships afloat. These graceful giants regularly crossed the Atlantic in four days. They are no longer in service, having been replaced by the Queen Elizabeth 2. So complicated are the day-to-day requirements of the modern liner that in this ship many of them are dealt with by a computer. It is the first of its kind to be installed in any merchant ship.

(1) The Queen Elizabeth 2
(2) An artist's impression of a nuclear-powered liner of the future

The Royal Merchant Navy

The ocean-going cargo liner runs to a fixed time-table between ports on a certain route. The tramp goes where cargo is to be found. The coaster carries goods on short voyages only.

The holds of a general cargo ship are like huge warehouses, and she is equipped with derricks to load and unload, though this is usually done by the cranes at the ports. Some cargo ships carry a small number of passengers as well as cargo.

Ships are designed specially for certain cargoes. The oil tanker has her engines and main superstructure aft, away from the highly inflammable oil in her tanks. Ships which carry meat, fruit, vegetables, or other perishable goods, have holds which are refrigerators. There is now a trend towards bigger bulk carrier ships. These have pipelines or conveyor belts for automatic loading and unloading of grain, sugar, chemicals, oil and other goods.

Great savings of manpower and shipping have been brought about by the use of the container ship. The containers are like huge packing cases filled with goods, usually at the factory. They can be stacked easily on the ship and need not be opened before reaching the customers abroad. The work of forty ordinary cargo ships can be done by five container ships in the same time.

A container ship and an oil tanker

The Fighting Ship

Fighting ships changed as weapons changed. Once the weapons were the bow and arrow, the spear and the sharp ram to sink the enemy ship. The invention of gunpowder brought cannon to ships, and stoutly built hulls to resist cannon balls. Ships sailed close in battle, fired broadsides at short range, ran together and grappled, and so fought it out.

The invention of rifled guns of long range, firing high explosive shells, changed the design of warships and the tactics of battle. The high-powered weapons, and scientific instruments, enabled ships to fight when they were miles apart.

The two world wars brought two new weapons, the submarine, which attacks with torpedoes when submerged, and the aeroplane. The aircraft carrier is a floating aerodrome, with a long, clear flight-deck made possible by setting the superstructure at the side, and hangars and workshops below decks. The aeroplanes are raised to the flight deck by lifts.

In the modern fighting ship, although the gun still is important, the guided missile has replaced it as the principal weapon. A Polaris submarine can carry sixteen missiles, giving it a fire power greater than all the bombs dropped by both sides during the second world war.

An aircraft carrier

The Fishing Fleets

Ships used for fishing vary in size and design according to the work they have to do. The deep sea trawlers go out all the year round, so they are powerful and sturdy vessels capable of staying at sea whatever the weather. The trawler drags a large cone-shaped net along the bottom of the sea, and hauls it in-board with derricks, called 'gallows'. The catch is sorted, gutted, and stored in ice in the hold.

The whale-catcher is a hunter; she is small, fast, and able to turn quickly when pursuing a whale. A harpoon gun is mounted in the bows, and a look-out spots the whales from his perch in the crow's nest.

A factory ship goes with the fleet of whale-catchers. She is a very large ship which carries fuel for the whale-catchers, and deals with the catch. The whales are towed to the factory ship, hauled on board up a slip-way, and cut up. The products are stored in the holds.

A good catch

The Sport of Sailing

The days of sail are not altogether finished. Small fishing boats still use sails, though they have a motor of some kind as well. They can be seen fishing off the coast, and a fine sight they are, too. It is fun to watch them coming into harbour with the motor chugging away, or perhaps coming in under sail, and to see the catch gleaming silver on the deck.

Sailing is best maintained, however, for pleasure, and our smaller harbours are crowded with private sailing yachts and motor boats. There are many yacht clubs, with their own moorings, a club-house, a boat yard, and regattas for racing.

Some people sail abroad to the Continent for their holidays in larger cabin yachts, while others cruise to distant parts of the world. The yacht is the ideal hobby for people who love the sea. Clubs hold regattas for children, who sail their little dinghies with great skill.

Special Ships

Special ships are designed for innumerable purposes. It is interesting to try to guess how a ship's construction has been designed for its task. You will notice, for example, that a tug always has her bridge and funnel set well forward, to leave as much space as possible aft for the towing cable. A dredger is easy to recognise; it is used to clear the channel in estuaries and rivers, and the entrance to harbours.

Weather ships perform a lonely duty, posted at scattered points about the oceans to report weather conditions for meteorological forecasts. Lightships have a lonely duty, too, though they are not always manned. They mark, with a flashing light at night, points of especial danger to shipping.

The most dramatic and courageous of all are, of course, the lifeboats. They are always ready to put to sea at the call of a ship in distress. Whatever the weather, whatever the peril, the coxswain and crew of a lifeboat never hesitate to put to sea on their errand of mercy.

Answering a call of S.O.S.

Ships of the future

Our story began with a log. As the new inventions and ideas came, so ships changed. From the log to the canoe with a paddle, and to the ship with oars. A sail was added, to help when the wind blew from astern. For many centuries there were no improvements, then the rudder was invented, and different arrangements of sails, so that the ship did not have to depend on a following wind.

A new era dawned with the steam engine, then steel hulls. The turbine, the motor and the diesel followed. Now we are on the brink of another great development, with the harnessing of atomic power to propel ships.

With this new source of energy a ship will be able to sail for very long periods of time without refuelling. Already submarines can perform the astonishing feat of encircling the world while remaining submerged. There is no doubt that sooner or later nuclear-powered ships will come into general use, and take their place in the long story which began with the log.

Nuclear-powered submarine

SAIL PLAN OF
FOUR-MASTED
BARQUE

Approx. 2,000 tons
Approx. 280′ long
Approx. 40′ beam
Cost about £29,000 in 1880

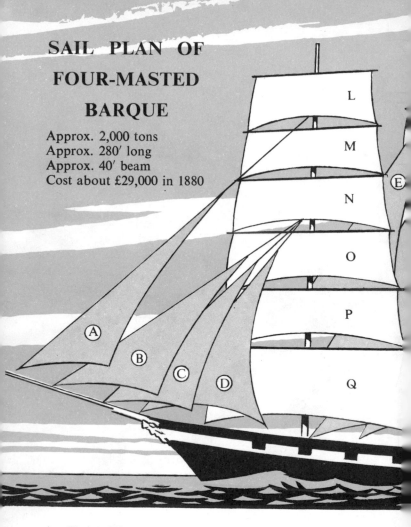

A	Flying Jib	**E**	Royal Stay-Sail
B	Outer Jib	**F**	Top-Gallant Stay-Sail
C	Inner Jib	**G**	Top-Mast Stay-Sail
D	Fore Top-Mast Stay-Sail	**J**	Jigger Stay-Sail